Ada's Grandma

A true story

A Biography of a Grandmother for Younger Readers

Published by **JUST CAUSE BOOKS**

103c Norwood Road Herne Hill
London
SE24 9AE

ISBN: 978-1-9997642-0-3

Ada's Grandma

A true story

A Biography of a Grandmother for Younger Readers

Chukwudum Ikeazor

TABLE OF CONTENTS

PHOTOGRAPHS

To

All Grandmas

Everywhere, anywhere and for all times

Introduction

On a cold evening in December 2007, just before Christmas, a little girl was born at the Emory Hospital in Atlanta, Georgia. Her father had just arrived that morning from England where he worked as a police officer. The baby girl was called Ada Maya Marina. She has grown into a chatty and curious little girl. When it came to questions, she was a natural! My name is Chukwudum. I am Ada's dad and I have to deal with her questions!

As she grew, she was very curious about her family. Her mother is American and so she has loads of uncles, aunts and cousins in the U.S. She has some uncles and quite a few cousins in Europe, after all her father and some family live there. But in Africa, in Nigeria, she had even more relatives, loads of them - grandparents, aunts, cousins and more cousins, after all her father is African. Some of these relatives had also travelled to other countries for work, study or to settle. This is how this little American girl, Ada and her kid brother Ikenna, came to have cousins and relatives all over the place; in England, Germany, South Africa, China, Sweden, etc.

One day, after answering so many questions about uncles, aunts and grandparents, especially her grandma Marina, whom she shares a name with, I agreed to write her a book about her grandma so she can read, and read again and again or have it read to her. Actually, I was working on a biography at the time when she demanded that a book be written for her too. So, this is how and why this grandma's biography for younger readers came to be written. I had never written before for younger readers so I struggled a lot and this was the best I could come up with. I admit that it has really turned out to be a book for not so young readers, but hope that Ada and other very young readers will get better grasp of the book as they grow. Still, it is a book that they can read and or have read to them by older readers who can also enjoy the book. I also hope that many young readers will encounter new words, ideas, concepts and other cultures here.

I hope that you enjoy this book and I hope that more books are written about grandmas and grandpas. I sure wish the one was written about my grandparents!

Chukwudum
London, 2017

Ada Maya Marina

The schoolgirl who got her dad to write her a book about her grandma.

Marina Chikezie
Ada's grandma, as a schoolgirl, in the early 1950s.

Foreword and HAPPY 80th BIRTHDAY message

This book is about my grandma, Marina Ikeazor, who will be 80 years old on 13 August 2017. On that day she will see this book for the first time. My daddy planned a special birthday surprise for her.

I thank my daddy for writing this book about my grandma. At first I was not sure if he was really going to write the book but the book is really here. I think this is a beautiful book and I love the pictures of grandma when she was younger and when she was a school girl. It is really nice to know her story from when she was a baby. Now I have it all in a book.

It is a very long book for children like me and there is a lot to read. There are some words there that I do not understand and have to look them up or ask. But it is okay since it is about my grandma and I get to learn some new words and new things too.

It is a book I will keep as I grow, as some parts of it really look like a grown up book, and I can read it better when I am older. I hope many little kids like me read and enjoy the book and learn new things too about grandmas, other people and other places.
My last message here is for you grandma.

This is for you on your 80th birthday. From me, my little brother Ikenna, my cousins, aunts, uncles, mommy and daddy and all our family there in Africa and here in America, and in England too –

HAPPY 80th BIRTHDAY !!!!!!!!

Ada Maya Marina Ikeazor

Atlanta, GA.
August 2017

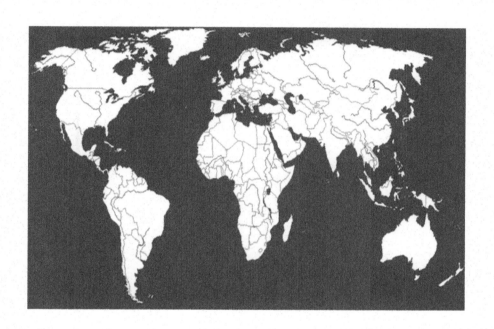

CHAPTER ONE

A World of Variety

Ada and her little brother, Ikenna, like little kids everywhere in the world love stories. They love family stories, Bible stories, stories about different places and people, fairy tales, history stories, stories from books, and made up and emergency stories, and I do my best to tell them stories as best as I could.

When Ada asked where her grandparents, uncles, aunts, and cousins on my side of her family lived, I would naturally tell her what countries they were at - Nigeria, England, Sweden and the United States as the case may be, but most were in Nigeria.

Every now and then there would be a phone call to or from any of them and she would speak with an assortment of relatives a number of whom she had never met – grandpa, grandma, this uncle or that aunt, and this or that cousin. But over time, one by one she began to meet some of her relatives on my side of the family, starting with when she came to England in 2010 and stayed with her grandma for a few months. When she got her first children's atlas I would point out the relevant countries and cities on the maps of Africa, Europe or North America where her relatives lived. These times were good opportunities for some short and quick geography lessons and quizzes in fun ways. In little or no time and at quite an early stage Ada could tell the capital cities of a few countries around the world.

I think it is right to start this book with something around our geography conversations and our one world as her grandmother's story touches on travel, geography and different parts of the world.

Every continent has people who are native to it or who have been there the longest and people who are either immigrants or whose families in the past came from other parts of the world either in the last few decades or even several hundreds of years ago. For example, in the USA and North America, Native Americans are the people who are native to America and have lived there for the longest and before all others such as the Europeans, Africans and Asians came or where brought there. I guess the term "Native American" is the giveaway.

13

From ancient times people have always moved around in search of food, trade, jobs or better life. This is normal. Some people are sometimes forced away from their homes because of war or other troubles there. This is not normal and is bad but these are still reasons why people move. Every immigrant or arriving community have their own stories.

Some people have sometimes been taken by force from their homes to other parts of the world where they did not want to go and forced to work against their will and without wages as enslaved persons. This is not normal and this was very wrong in the past and is very wrong today. There is no excuse for it. Some people are forced to move because of natural disasters like famines, floods or earthquakes.

The story of the world is one of continuous movement of peoples and this is often called migration. Because of this, every continent and most countries in the world are a mix of people from different parts of the world and other countries. Every country in the world has been affected by migration. We are all mixed in one way or the other. This is sometimes called diversity.

The planet, Earth, is the only home that humans have and all humans are connected; by travel, history, and heritage. Diversity can be a good thing because it can make things varied, colourful and exciting. Smart and sensible people respect our different and diverse natures and stories. They know that many of these differences are not reasons at all for arguments, fights or treating any person differently.

We are so merrily mixed. Some children have parents from two different countries or cultures. Some have parents with different religions. In fact, diversity is natural and is all around us. Some have a tall parent and a very short one, a white parent and a black one, an English dad and a Chinese mum, an African father and an Asian mother, or a German mother and a Canadian father and so on and so on. Ada is American but her grandmother is African. Ada is American but her dad is a Briton. Her dad is a Briton, but he is also an African. Her mother has African-American grandparents as she is African American, but her mother also has a Native American grandparent.

All these differences in appearance, heritage, experience, tastes and so on are not problems at all. They make us interesting and diverse. It will be quite boring and quite weird if we all looked the same, talked the same way, and liked the same things. In a sense, thank heavens for our diversity.

It is sad, however, that for some people, diversity seems to be problem but the truth is that it is they who are the problem and not diversity. Diversity is part of nature even for those who appear to have problems with it.

We all cannot and do not all look alike or like the same things. We do not all look at or see things the same the way. Life is diverse and as the saying goes, "variety is the spice of life".

Throughout history and to this day, differences or the diversity of how we look, our race, our religions, ethnicities, nationalities, our views about how we should live, have caused wars and the oppression of one group by another.

Some countries have been trying to learn from their past and have taken steps and made laws to protect people from discrimination because of these differences. The United Kingdom and the United States are some of those countries that have made such laws and policies. Discrimination and disputes about these differences do not suddenly stop or vanish because laws have been made, but at least it is a start and people who break those laws can be punished.

The vast majority of people, however, know that diversity is variety, natural and can be fun; and they get along with people from any background, community, country or religion happily.

CHAPTER TWO

A Little Girl in Gudi - Nigeria

Now, the story of Marina starts right from the little town where she was born. Gudi is a quiet, lively town high up in the table land or the plateau areas of Northern Nigeria, in Nassarawa State. The air there is clean and brisk; well, it was when Marina was born. A rail line runs through the town taking people and goods from one part of the country to another.

It is one of the most important towns in the locality as it has a train station. This attracts a lot of people, business and traffic. In the town, there are traders, craftspeople, old people, young people, school children, students, Christians, Muslims, and people from different parts of Nigeria. In Gudi, like some parts of Nigeria, there are different languages spoken, perhaps as many as ten by people from different communities.

In townships and cities, people usually come from other places, some near and some far, to settle to trade, work, or look for work. In countries like Nigeria and many others such as India, Ghana, Kenya, or South Africa they may come from other parts of the country where other languages are spoken. This may not be the case in places like France, England, Mexico or the United States, where generally one language is spoken by everyone except perhaps immigrants. In some parts of the USA, English and Spanish are generally spoken too.

In the case of these countries and cities where people speak so many different languages, it would have been quite difficult for everyone to understand everyone else on the streets, in schools, markets and shops and so on and so the answer lay in one or two common languages. In northern Nigeria where Gudi is, many people there learned and still learn to speak English and/or Hausa, a northern Nigerian language, as well as their own languages. The results were that anyone there could converse and communicate with everyone else and many people could speak two or three languages.

It is very much like a London or New York neighborhood where you may find some Bengalis, Colombians, Chinese, Nigerians, Polish and other folks, all of whom have their own ethnic or national languages but all have to speak English to communicate with each other and members of the wider community, as English is the national language or lingua franca in England.

It was in Gudi a very long time ago, on Friday 13 August 1937 that a little girl named Marina was born. Her names were Marina and Chikezie but everyone called her Marina. She was the second child of Benson and Elizabeth Onyire, who came from the town of Obosi, in southern Nigeria. Benson was the Railway Station master in Gudi. He looked after the passengers at the station, the train drivers and guards and told people when the next train was due and where the trains were going. He managed the station workers such as the clerk or clerks, guard, cleaners and anyone else who helped out there. He was a very important man in the small town of Gudi and everyone knew him.

Marina was his second child. His first child was also a girl. He was happy with his little girls but he also wanted a boy too. Of course, boys and girls are equally important, but for some reasons in some parts of the world many people want boy children more than they want girl children. In fact, Benson had wanted a boy as his first child like many families then and even now. So, he and his wife Elizabeth kept having more children, hoping for a boy child. Benson may have said to himself "I want a boy child. I want a son so that my line and name will continue. When he grows up he can go to college or university, get a good job and make me proud." He would have prayed to God to give him a boy child and his wife Elizabeth would have prayed even harder too as she wanted to make her husband happier by giving birth to a baby boy.

They had another child and it was a girl yet again. Young Benson was getting very impatient now. Benson so wanted a boy and he thought that if he had another wife he would have a boy. Maybe he thought that it was his wife's fault that he had no boy-child. Many people think this way, but of course it is not anyone's fault. It is not a fault to have just boys or girls. It is just a matter of chance, like many things in life. Well, after having three girls in a row, Benson married another wife, apparently in his quest for a boy. He did not divorce Elizabeth as under Nigerian customs a married man could marry again and again and have several wives at the same time. This is called polygamy.

In many parts of Africa and Asia men could marry more than one wife. It is not so common now but it was then, and still happens in many places today. Interestingly, women were not allowed to have more than one husband at a time! Anyway, Benson eventually had more children, including boys and more girls. He even married one more wife. He loved his girls but he desperately wanted a boy because in his culture it is thought that boys were more important than girls. But this is wrong because really girls and boys are equal and just as important as the other. In many parts of the world today there are people who think that boys are more important than girls. Girls and boys are just as important and the world cannot work without the other.

Girls and boys are part of the family in the same way. They are a part of the community and every country in the same way and they all contribute to their families, communities and the countries. Little boys grow up to become prime ministers or presidents in many countries. Little girls grow up to become prime ministers or presidents in some countries too, but certainly not anywhere as many as boys do. Still, in countries like Sri Lanka, Bangladesh, Brazil, Pakistan, India, Germany, Finland, Israel, England, Iceland, Liberia, Argentina women have become prime ministers and presidents. Maybe, this could be the case too in America soon.

When Marina was growing up she could not have ever thought of becoming a president or even a lawyer or doctor. Girls generally did not grow up to become such things in her part of the world then. They just did some little schooling, grew up, got married and had their own family and became wives and mothers. Some lucky ones could become nurses, teachers, clerks, market or market women. In some parts of Northern Nigeria then, some girls did not even do any schooling at all. They were not encouraged or allowed to go to any schools or even learn how to read and write by their families and communities.

It was quite a different world then for women all over the world. In most countries, women were not encouraged or allowed to hold important jobs. In 1937, when Marina was born, there was no female prime minister or president ever in the world. The business of running countries was left just to men. At the time she was born, Nigeria was a British colony and it was governed by British officials with the help of some Nigerians and all these people were men. They were the ones who had education mostly.

19

Happily, this has changed very much today and more and more girls are encouraged to go to school, at least primary school. There is, however, some work to do there and in many parts of the world as there are some people who still think that girls should not be educated. In 2012 a schoolgirl called Malala was shot in the head in Pakistan by some men who wanted to kill her because they thought that little girls should not go to school. It sounds crazy but it happened. Young Malala Yousafzai, survived. She was flown to England for treatment and now lives there with her family. Her country Pakistan is not safe for her. In a way, she is now a refugee. She is also a powerful and international campaigner for girls' education and is a Nobel Prize winner.

In Marina's time as a young girl and in her country, things were not as bad as that at all and she did go to school with no danger, even though she did not go on to college or university. Like in many parts of Africa and Asia, Marina's family was big and family meant not just parents and siblings but cousins, aunts, uncles and grandparents. Everyone was involved with everyone else and they all looked out for each other. Marina loved to play with her siblings, cousins and friends at home and at school. They did not have the sort of toys that kids in England or America would be familiar with like toy cars, train sets or dolls but kids in Nigeria made up their own toys from pieces of wood and tin cans and so on.

They also played the sort of games that kids all over the world would play - football (Americans call it soccer), hide and seek, hop-skip-jump, pretend cooking and so on. They held racing and jumping competitions, sang, danced, played mom and dad and so on. They were just like kids everywhere else. Marina was a bright pupil in her class and her father and mother were very proud of her. When she first started school she used slates and white chalk for her lessons like all her class mates. They wrote on the black slates with the white chalks. Slates were small and handheld. They were like portable blackboards on which the children wrote, with white chalks and did their class work. They could and would be wiped clean with a duster or piece of cloth and readied for next lesson.

As the school children got older and moved up in grades they started using pencils and exercise books and then pens. Their schools had no libraries but their parents could buy books for them. Books were very

20

precious items and were treated with great care and handed down to younger siblings or friends. The teacher would write on a big blackboard with white chalks. The kids learned to count with pebbles and times tables. There were no calculators, computers or internet then. These were still a long way ahead in the future.

Marina and her family lived in Gudi for a few years but later went to another city called Enugu. There she went to a school called St. Bartholomew's Primary School. Everyone called the school "St Baths". When she was about 10 years old her father sent her to the Holy Ghost Convent School at the big market city, Onitsha. The school was run by Catholic nuns from a faraway country, Ireland. They were called the Irish Sisters because they were from Ireland. They also had some Igbo teachers.

Marina's favourite teacher was Miss Martha, an Igbo woman from a nearby town called Ogidi. The school was a boarding school which meant that the school children lived there during school term. While at the school Marina joined the Girls Guide because she loved their activities, games and the sense of belonging to a group.

The teachers in the schools were very strict and were very good. They took great pride in the success of any of their students and worked hard to get them to succeed. They also worked their pupils hard. In those days, teachers had a lot of power and prestige and were highly respected in the community. They had the sort of powers and respect that teachers had in Victorian England or in America in the 19th century which was in many cases a lot of power and authority.

They readily used the cane, which is the stick, on any pupil when they thought it was needed. This was very Victorian too. A pupil who refused to follow instructions or even failed tests and times tables too often could be punished with some strokes of the cane. This was very normal in those days and the children's parents were quite happy with it. No child would think of complaining to their parent that they got punished at school because they would probably get punished again by their parents for being naughty at school. Marina was a good student and for the most part avoided punishment by doing what she was supposed to do and at the right time too.

She was not sure what she wanted to be when she grew up but she worked hard at her studies. She might have sometimes thought she wanted to be a teacher like Miss Martha because she was a role model to them. In those days folks had never seen or known of any girl who grew

21

up to became a doctor, lawyer, accountant, airline pilot, or the boss of a company, but many or most girls grew up to become housewives and mothers. They may also have a market stall business or work in the farm for or with their husbands, or sell food, but that was that. And so, little girls in the world in which Marina grew up simply did not speak of growing up to be doctors, lawyers, airline pilots or scientists and the like.

The same was for jobs like being an engineer, train driver, post person, or even a Railway Station Master like Marina's father. Because of the situation, folks generally just thought that those jobs were for men and that little girls could only grow up and expect to be market-women, farmers, nurses and may be teachers.

When Marina finished her convent school education, she wanted to go to High School and learn more things but she was only to be very disappointed. Her father made her understand that she already had enough education for a girl. She could now read, write and speak English and that was enough! She and other girls in the family and indeed the community were made to understand that higher education especially going to university was reserved for boys.

One or the main reason given for this by some men in Marina's part of the world at that time was that girls got married and moved away into their husbands' homes (and changed their last names to their husbands') but boys will stay with the family or in the family home and would always keep the family name. In other parts of Nigeria and parts of the world, another of the reasons behind this behaviour towards girls lay in religion, as some people think that God wants girls to grow up and just be good wives and mothers and do nothing else other than mothering, cooking, cleaning at home. If they had to work they were expected to be farmers, market women or traders, dress makers and not ever take jobs that required them to be very educated. This attitude was more prevalent in some of the Northern parts of Nigeria where they were Muslims.

There were all sorts of reasons all over the place including Europe and America (in the past) but none of these reasons made sense and none was fair. Boys and girls have equal rights to education to any level. Marina's father explained that he was saving up his money for his boys' education at college and university and that his daughters would be getting married anyway.

Marina was not very happy but was an obedient child and accepted what she was told. In any case, all around her no girl was going to university so it seemed almost normal. She then stayed in the house and helped her mother around the house and helped her younger siblings with their lessons. She was also learning to be a good mother and a good wife by watching her mother closely and following her advice and instructions just like girls all over the country did.

Helping at home meant doing all sorts of chores in the house and some fetching from outside. At home, little girls and little boys, after school, would help their parents keep the house clean, go to the woods usually with adults to fetch firewood for cooking and or go the stream to fetch water for cooking and bathing.

There was no electricity in most parts of Africa in the 1930s and 1940s and no tap or pipe-borne water in many villages and homes. Cooking was usually done on tripod stands with firewood burning beneath. Firewood may be bought from some sellers in town or would have to be collected in the woods and forests and brought back home. They would be tied together in bundles and carried on the head sometimes for miles. As there was no running water in many homes, in some towns there would be public taps in a square, field or major street corner. Children and adults would walk there from their homes, line up for their turns or sometimes fight their way through and fill their pails (buckets) with water and then carry them on their heads them home.

Some towns such as Onitsha, Markurdi and Lokoja were built by huge rivers and folks also fetched water from the rivers. So while they had pipe-borne water, some folks also had access to the river! This was the way it was in the 1930s when Marina was born and much the same in her teens in the early 1950s. In villages, the water supplies were always streams or springs. Children and adults would to go to streams to bathe and wash clothes and fetch water back to the homes for cooking and other uses, including home bathing. Older folks did not have to go to the river unless they wanted to and younger people in the family would bring back water for them for their use.

Children were seen as helpers in the house. Marina and her siblings helped their parents in the house too. When it came to the kitchen, it was usually the girls that helped. As they helped, they learned how to cook from their mothers and this way, it was seen as the woman's business to know how to cook for the family and little girls started learning how to cook very early. When they were big enough they too could actually also cook for their family.

23

The boys usually learned how to fish, hunt, wrestle and fight and doing things which were considered to be boys' and men's business. They would also learn many skills, outlooks for life and sometimes learn trades from their fathers. For families that had enough money, the boys would be encouraged to study very hard to go to college and in some cases, to university.

Of course, anyone can cook and any one can fish or hunt whether they are male or female but there are many roles that societies assign to women or to men separately. This has been the case in every society in the world for centuries, but today some societies, especially in Europe and America, no longer mind what men or women do in the house or at work. In smart and modern households, everyone helps with the house chores. Mums and dads cook, clean and babysit as necessary.

In many African and Asian countries, one of the important duties in the house for older children was looking after their younger siblings or cousins, from the babies, toddlers and really young ones. They would help with their feeding, cleaning up, bathing and generally looked after them to ensure they were safe. This was how it was in Marina's world. There was no day care and sometimes no nurseries and family and neighbours looked after each other's children. Sometimes, a live-in help or baby sitter would be hired to help the family.

When Marina was older and her parents had more children, she had to do her bit too. She may have been as young as seven or even six when she started helping out. She took care of her younger siblings and they all looked up to her. When the ones she looked after grew older, they helped out with the ones younger than them and so on and so on. This was the way it was all over Africa. Marina's parents had live-in house helps

In Marina's house and everywhere else, the children played too and had great open spaces for playing. Most houses in villages had large front gardens often referred to as compounds and every village had a square which was open to everyone. In townships and urban areas, these spaces were referred to as "Yards".

The children played games that children anywhere would recognise - hide and seek, hop skip jump, clap songs and rhyming songs, sports, competitive racing and of course football, which Americans call soccer. The boys would wrestle and sometimes go fishing or hunting in local streams and forests. In those days there were no televisions sets, no movie houses and certainly no computer games so what would Marina and other children do when it got dark?

After readying themselves for the next day the children would gather round an adult to be told fairy tales or ancestral stories about how their families or communities came to be. Some of the stories even came with sing-songs which the children joined. These tales were usually told by an older family member - mum, dad or grandparents or uncle and aunts. Some of these storytellers were favoured.

This was how the stories of many African peoples have been preserved, told from generation to generation. It is called oral history. There are some parts of Africa where there are specialists who know the history of their communities by heart going back several generations. These people are called griots. When many Africans were taken forcible to the Americas in the 17th, 18th and part of the 19th centuries to work as slaves, many of them kept memories of their homelands alive through stories which were handed down from generation to generation. One of the most famous of these stories was retold by Alex Hailey in his book, Roots. This was later made into a movie.

Some of the stories Marina and other children listened to at the feet of their parents or some older relative were about the tortoise, an animal that folk-lore considered to be very clever and cunning, always running rings round other animals and people. Some of the stories were very spooky and would scare the children very much but they loved the stories anyway. They also had Cinderella- like stories too, sad stories that had happy endings.

The stories were not all fairy tales. Family elders also told stories about the family and town history. They told about their local heroes from the past and present; who the ancestors were, where they came from and when. The children would listen with rapt attention, prompting the storyteller with questions here and there. They learnt the stories by heart and when they could tell their younger siblings stories too in no time.

As they gathered round in the evening or night time, depending on the season, they could be enjoying natural snacks of roast corn cobs and pear, coconut or peeled oranges. Sometimes when there was full moon, there was sufficient light to see around in the open in the compound or in the square. It was of course not enough to read or do many things people do during the day but it was enough.

During moonlit nights and especially on weekends, parents could let older children go out and play in the compound or to the village square with other children. There could sing songs, dance, play hide and seek or hold poetry and proverb competitions. There was always so much to do and the children were never ever bored. The children and the families did not miss television because they never had any and they were able to keep themselves very busy and active. They did not have toy shops to go to but they could make themselves toys from many things.

After school hours and after having their meals and doing their home chores, children had time for many things. They could play games in the front yard, do their homework, and or practice their times tables and spelling. They would also help out at home, helping their mother prepare meals. By helping their mothers cook, the girls learned how to cook as time went by. Sometimes the children would go to fetch more water from the nearest stream or public tap. Americans call taps faucets.

In the 1930s and 1940s most homes in Nigeria did not have taps or faucets where people get water whenever the needed. Children and adults had to go to wells, streams or rivers to fetch water which they carried back home on their heads in gourds, pots and pails. Some wells were near homes or actually within the home compounds but some and the rivers could be quite a distance from home. Today, in many parts of Africa, apart from areas where very rich folks live, there is water shortage and many people have to walk some distance to get water to use at home. It can be tough but it is what they have to do and children who were big enough to walk and carry things on their heads were expected to help too.

At Marina's home and during her childhood, education was very important and children had to do well or pass their examinations. Their parents paid for their education and even at primary school, not doing well in school was like wasting your parents' money. In many parts of Africa, children who did not do well in their tests or failed to pass what they called term examinations do not go to the next class or grade the following year.

It was important for the children to help their parents out by doing well in school. Marina was very bright and always pleased her parents with her good grades. She enjoyed going to school and did well in all her grades at primary school and convent school (not proper nouns as they are not specific names). So, it was very sad for her when she was told that she could not go to school any more. She knew she would have to be married soon as that was the next major step in life for teenage girls.

Anyway, not going to school did not stop her from reading or helping others learn to read and write. She kept herself occupied with any books she could lay her hands on and helped her younger siblings and neighborhood children with their lessons after school. She would also help adults and older people who had no reading skills by reading their letters for them or any written information that they wanted to understand, such as newspapers. She was pretty busy learning and as she grew.

In a short while her life would change in the way it was hoped for and expected of girls and young women then. She and her family would receive a marriage proposal for her and her family to consider.

CHAPTER THREE

Marriage, England and Motherhood

When Marina turned 16 her family and the family of a certain young man met and agreed that they should marry. Marina and the young man had to be asked if would like to be married to each other and they said "yes". They knew themselves as their families were from the same town, Obosi.

One day, she had come back home from the market and her father called her into the living room; "Marie, bia (come)". "Yes, sir", she replied. In those days children addressed their parents very respectfully. She ran to see her father who was with some relatives. He said to her. "There are some people who have come to ask after you". She knew what that meant.

A young man's family had come to express interest in her for marriage on behalf of the young man. Her face went to the floor immediately in shyness. She said little more. Her father went on. "Oh ndi be Ikeazor (It is the Ikeazors)". She knew straight away who it was.

This was one of her chances to say "no" but she stayed respectfully silent, in agreement to the proposal. She knew the young man in question from a few years ago. He was the one who had gone to England to go to university. Everyone in the neighborhood knew him even if they had not all met him. His story was all over the place. He had gone to England, to the Queen's country! They called England "Obodo Oyibo", that is "The white people's country". Only very few people had been to England then and those who did were treated like local celebrities by some people.

Marina's suitor's father was a senior police officer in the Nigeria Police Force. It was quite a thing in those days for an African to be in that kind of position. He was in charge of many police officers including some English men who were in the Nigerian Police Force then. He had been to England and trained at famous police colleges at Hendon and Bramshill. He was famous in the entire region. He later became one of the first Africans to become a Commissioner of Police in all of Africa.

Marina's mind was all over the place. She was excited, scared, sad, happy, unsure, and so on. Later that evening Marina's mother would speak with her and ask her again if she was all right with the marriage proposal. She was only 16 or 17. Marrying and raising a family was what everyone was expected to do and finding a person you liked, to propose to or be proposed to was a happy event.

Marina knew Timothy before he left for England as his mother lived nearby. She thought he was a very handsome and clever young man. What she did not know was that after he left for England he had been thinking about her and secretly adored her. When he started discussing marriage with his parents, his mind went to that young girl he last saw in Nigeria a couple of years earlier. But of course, he could not start writing her, dating her or just propose to her directly. Their families had to be involved. They had to make and receive the proposals and come to agreements that the marriage could take place and then obtain the consent of the young woman in question. That was how it was done in those days in Nigeria and in many parts of Africa. It is still so in some parts today. In those days, there was no dating or partying. Marriages were very much arranged and agreed by families. This also happens in many parts of Asia.

Arranged marriage involves discussions and agreements between families, but this only went ahead if the couple agreed to be married. It was always the man and his family who would propose to the girl and her family. She had to agree and so did her parents. There was no force at all.

Arranged marriage is different from forced marriage where young girls are forced into marriage by their parents or family. This is clearly wrong and in some countries like England, people can be sent to prison for forcing any young girl or young boy to marry. Nobody should ever be forced to marry someone against her or his will.

Marina was glad to be getting married to her future husband, and the choice her parents had made for her in accepting his family's proposal. He was a very educated man. He had been a teacher and was now studying overseas. Any country or land that you had to cross the seas to get to was referred to generally as "overseas" by Nigerians and Africans in those days.

After some Igbo marriage ceremonies and feasts, a lot of preparations and many tearful farewells, Marina left to meet her husband. In the spring of 1955 she flew with a jetliner from Lagos, Nigeria to London, England where her husband lived. It was her first time in an airplane and she was a little scared but was too excited to be scared all the time. She was also travelling with another young friend from her hometown Obosi who was also going to meet her husband in England.

Marina's husband was 7 years older than her. His full name was Timothy Chimezie. Then everyone called him Timo. He was excited at meeting his young bride at Heathrow Airport near London and took some of his friends with him to receive her. They fell in love and married at an old church in London called St. Margaret's. They became Mr. and Mrs. Ikeazor. They went for their honeymoon in a little seaside town called Shanklin on the Isle of Wight on the south coast of England. They lived in a part of London called Wandsworth at No. 270 Trinity Road.

Marina settled to life in London but she missed her mother, father and siblings very much. London was quite a sight for her - the big and red double decker buses, the underground trains that is, subway to Americans and Metro to the French, and the very tall buildings like she had never seen or imagined before. Although she liked London very much, she did not like the cold and always dressed very warmly when she went out.

On Tuesday, the 11th of September 1956 Marina gave birth to her first child, a baby boy. He was a plump little thing with fat cheeks and a head full of hair. Timo became a very proud father and was very excited that his family was now three in number, him, Marina and the new baby. They gave him three very long African names, but we shall stick with just one here. He was called *Chukwudum*. The name means *"God Guide(s) me"* in the Igbo language.

It was very unusual in those days for African children in England to be baptised with only African names. They all had to have one English name or a name from the Bible and one African name, but his daddy a proud young African man insisted and so little Chukwudum became one of the first African children in England to have only African names. He was not going to be called, Tom, Dick or Harry, or Peter, Paul or John. He was Chukwudum. It was this plump baby with fat cheeks, and a head full of hair that would one day grow up to become Ada's and Ikenna's dad.

The house the Ikeazors lived in was owned by a Welsh woman, a widow, who was about the same age as Marina's mother. She was their landlady and her name was Joan Battershill. She was a very friendly and kindly lady. When Marina was getting home sick and was missing her mother Joan Battershill told her that she would be her mother while she

31

was in England. Joan said to the young Marina, "I know your mother is back in Africa and you miss her a lot but if you let me, I will be your mum while you are in England, Ok?" Marina agreed.

Joan had never been to Africa before and this was Marina's first time in Europe. She was Welsh and Marina was Igbo. She was a much older Welsh lady and Marina a teenage African girl. None of these mattered at all and the two women became great friends. When she had her new baby, Joan Battershill was there for Marina giving her advice and support. Joan was so kind that she let the young family stay in her house for a couple of years without taking any rent money from them. As we shall discover later, the young Ikeazors, never forgot this.

In London in those days there were not very many Africans in London then but there were quite a few. Most who where there were students on their own or sometimes with their young families. Then Nigeria did not have a university and so many Nigerians like many other Africans came to England to study to become doctors, lawyers, accountants, engineers or to have university degrees. There were also people from other parts of the world whose countries were or had been colonies of England. Many of them came from countries in Africa, Asia and the Caribbean to study or work. Some Nigerians and Africans also went to the United States to study. Nigeria's first President, Nnamdi Azikiwe, went to Howard University in Washington DC and Lincoln University in Pennsylvania in the 1930s. Kwame Nkrumah, Ghana's first Prime Minister and President, also went to Lincoln University.

There were other young women like Marina from Nigeria and other parts of Africa who came who came to meet their husbands. Marina made friends with some of these, especially those from Nigeria. In London, she got a job as a trainee nurse to learn how to be a nurse and also make some money while her husband studied at university. She liked working in the hospital because she liked helping and meeting people. She also had a chance to meet other people from other parts of England and the world. She loved her smart student nurse's uniform.

By the time she left England a few years later, she was a mother of two little boys, her husband was a lawyer, and she had made many friends and learned many new things. She was now a married mother and had achieved what was expected of her as a young girl. She left Nigeria four years earlier as Miss Marina Onyire and returned as Mrs. Marina Ikeazor, a lawyer's wife and the mother of his two children.

32

Marina with her new family

– Her husband Timo and her baby, Chukwudum – 1956

Marina's six:
Top – the first four, at Onitsha, 1966
Bottom – the last two, at Lagos, 1974

CHAPTER FOUR

Back to Africa - Nigeria

In 1957 Marina returned to Nigeria to give her baby to his grandmother to look after and to give birth to her second child, Philip Emeka. It was normal practice for some young couples to leave their babies with the children's grandparents so they could concentrate on their studies. Many young African couples in England placed their children with foster parents so they could study or work. In Marina's case she took Chukwudum back to Nigeria to his grandmother.

After about a year's stay in Nigeria, she left her two little sons in their grandmother's care and returned to England to be with and help her husband. While he studied and went for his lectures at university, she worked to bring in some extra money and kept home, washing, cleaning and cooking. She also helped him with his revisions and organising his homework. As she worked to earn some money, her husband did not have to worry too much about money. He could pay more attention to his studies in other to pass his tests and examinations. Their parents sent them money from Nigeria, but sometimes they had run out before the money arrived.

Marina would have liked to study again get some qualifications or go to university but this was not practical. They were sometimes short on money like students were and they could not afford the time or the money for her to go back into full time education.

In any case, they were a team and as Timo was studying to become a lawyer and she was his wife. She had a big stake in his success too. When he becomes a lawyer, she can become a lawyer's wife and that was seen as a very important status too for women in those days. If they could not be somebody important in the society, at least they could be an important person's wife. In those days, there were very few women lawyers in the UK, US or the world for that matter and there was none in Nigeria.

Today, that has changed very much and there are very many women lawyers all over the world. A woman does not need to settle for a lawyer husband in order to have status, she can easily be a lawyer herself. One of the most famous female lawyers in the world today is Hillary Clinton, the former American First Lady and former Secretary of State. In the 2016 US election, she very nearly became the president. As for Marina and lawyers, one of her daughters (Sharon) and one of her younger sisters (Uche) are lawyers.

When Timo finished his studies and became a lawyer, he and Marina went back to their country just in time for its independence in 1960. They sailed on a passenger ship called MV Auriol from England, passing by the coasts of France, Spain, and Portugal in Europe until they reached the west of Africa. They were in the Atlantic Ocean for about two weeks until they arrived Lagos, then the capital of Nigeria.

In Nigeria, Timo, after working for the government in Lagos for a short while, set up practice as a lawyer. The Ikeazors moved to a town called Onitsha, a big bustling place, full of people. It had the biggest market in West Africa and was at the banks of the great River Niger, the longest and biggest river in West Africa. Two countries, Niger Republic and Nigeria take their names after it.

By 1967 they had six children. Timo said he loved children because he was his mother's only child. The children's names were Chukwudum, Emeka, Nwamaka, Sharon, Nonso and Chimezie. The first two were boys, the second two girls and the last two boys.

Marina's husband was now a practicing lawyer and an important man in the community. Marina was not going to work as such but she had what was really the most job in human history. She had a job or role that millions and millions of women had but it was not really called a job. She was a mother! She took care of the children, helped to get them ready for school, took them to after school lessons, cooked for them and taught them how to be good people. She was a full time mother and a housewife.

She had some help in the house as she had a lot of children. There were house helps who were paid and sometimes some relatives who came to stay and help out. African families worked like that. You were never ever alone in Africa and could hardly ever be lonely. Family members helped each other out in farms, in businesses, at homes and so on. This is the way it is in many parts of Africa and Asia. At Onitsha, families like others in other parts of the province did things together, went to church together, and celebrated festivals together. This was exactly the same in other parts of Nigeria – Calabar, Jos, Ibadan, Kaduna, Benin, and Lagos and so on.

Sundays were always special days. First, it was a weekend day and second they went to church, and third, it was also a day that many people visited families and friends or received them. The church was a big centre of family gathering for praying, singing and meeting. The children would be dressed in their "Sunday best". Some churches had Sunday Schools for children where they learned about God, Jesus and the Bible and sang.

Marina and her husband wanted all their children to go to university. Even when they were children, Chukwudum and his siblings knew they were expected to go to university and join a profession. All the boys and all the girls knew that and they knew that they had to do well in their examinations even from primary school. They had the example of their father, uncles and aunts to look up to. Their mother always told them that they can do whatever they liked when they grew up but that they must first put education in their pockets and that included university degrees.

The children were encouraged to work hard and well in their studies by a number of reasons. When they did well in school, their parents praised them and got them more presents. The children also knew that good school results pleased their parents and those happy parents were easier to get pocket money and other favours from. They, like many children, liked making their parents happy and proud and liked being praised. They loved school too as they had very many friends to play with there and their school had a great library where they could read and borrow books from.

When some, like Chukwudum, struggled with some subjects like mathematics, Marina organised after school classes for them. She would take them to the special classes after school, check their homework and continue to encourage them.

She also bought them loads and loads of story books for them to enjoy and work on their reading and spelling. On some evenings or some Saturdays, she would drive them to the town's public library or have a driver take them there. In those days in Onitsha, there were very few female drivers so sometimes people and other drivers stared at her. Education was extremely important to her. She wanted to see her denied dreams fulfilled through her children. She did not make a great deal of noise or do any drama about this but in her own quiet way she worked for her dreams for her children.

The period was now in the mid-1960s and her parents were now retired and lived in their hometown, Obosi, which was about 3 miles from Onitsha. She visited them very often and also continued to pay attention to her siblings' education, especially the girls. She ensured that all her sisters and half-sisters were continuing with their education as far as they desired or could. She encouraged them not to even think of marrying in their teens and to think of their education first.

She would say to them things like "a good education will help you get good jobs and even good husbands" and also that "Good education will open your eyes or shine the light for you, so that you don't walk around in the dark". The girls believed her and all of them studied hard and went to high schools and some did go on to universities. She and Timo helped her father with school fees for her sisters every now and then. This was quite normal. She was big sister and the first daughter. Her cousins and distant cousins also came to her and her husband expecting financial help with school fees or other costs.

This was the way African extended families worked. People helped each other and those who had more money than others were expected to help those who were poor or poorer.

By 1965, one of her sisters Edna had gained admission to university to study medicine. After her High School, she had suitors who wanted to marry her. Her father was quite happy as they were wealthy men or from rich families, but Marina put her foot down. As the Ada, (first daughter) she had a lot of influence in the family and as the wife of a very important man she even had more.

Education first for her sister. *"Edna ga eje lili university"*, Edna must go to university, she said. She and her husband got some money together towards Edna's fees and her father also got onboard too. She gave her sister many of her own clothes, helped her pack and off she went to Ibadan where the university was.

Life was happy for Marina, her husband and her children at Onitsha but their peace and happiness were about to be greatly disturbed. By 1967, she had turned 30. The next two years would be some of the most difficult years for Marina and millions of people in her part of Nigeria. There was trouble brewing in some parts of the country. Big trouble!

Marina's friend and landlady in London, Joan Battershill during her visit to Nigeria in 1973. The little boy with her is Chimezie, Marina's last child.

Marina with her husband, six children, her sister Uche, left back row, and their dog Noddy, in Lagos in the mid-seventies.

CHAPTER FIVE

The Biafran Journey (Life as Refugees)

In Nigeria in the early 1960s, there had been quite a lot of disagreement between politicians (that is the governors, premier, senators, president and prime minister) from different parts of the country for quite some time. One day in Nigeria in January 1966 some soldiers rebelled and staged what they called a revolution against the government.

There was plenty of shooting and some soldiers and government officials, including some senior army officers, premiers and the Prime Minister were killed. For the rest of the year there was trouble in that land and several thousands of people were killed as a result. Many countries often have difficult and violent times in their history and Nigeria was and is one of those so affected in recent times.

In 1967 things got worse and a war broke out. The world came to know this as the Biafran war. Timo, Marina and their children and millions of other people from their part of Nigeria became known as Biafrans. Marina, her husband and their six children with many relatives fled their homes for safety in other parts of Biafra as the war came closer. War is always a terrible thing as many people get killed and injured and many lose their homes too.

Life in Biafra was tough. Because of the war, food was short. There was no electricity so there were no more televisions or refrigerators. In the night they had to see with oil lamps. Everything became much more expensive and for many folks money was always short. Virtually everything was short and there was much hunger and starvation in the land. For quite some time, the schools were shut down because many had been destroyed by bombs and many teachers had gone off to become soldiers or were killed.

The Nigerian soldiers called Marina's people rebels but Marina's people called themselves Biafrans. The Nigerians said they were rebelling, but the Biafrans said they were fighting for their independence, much in the same way that George Washington and others said they were fighting and did fight for American independence.

The war, like in many wars resulted from disputes between politicians, soldiers and very rich and powerful people. The Nigerian political disputes and the Army mutiny of January 1966 led to riots and pogroms. During those riots and pogroms, thousands of people, many who spoke the same language as Marina did and were, like her Christians, were killed.

This was called a massacre. Marina's people, from the eastern part of the country did not feel safe in Nigeria anymore. They wanted their own country where they could run their lives in the way they chose and where they could be safe. They wanted their independence, in the way colonies or oppressed people can sometimes want their independence or their own country.

Other people around the world who had wanted and for the most part achieved their independence or their own country include the United States, Eritrea, East Timor, Bangladesh, Ghana, Sri Lanka, Jamaica, The Republic of Ireland and several other countries in Africa and Asia that were once colonies of European nations. During Biafran war, more and more people were killed and many more died from starvation. The story of the Biafran war was all over the news and televisions across the world during this time, the late 1960s.

As the war came closer to their home at Onitsha, Marina and her husband and six children packed into their small Nsu Prinz car with as many of their things as they could carry and drove away. They left behind their home furnishings, television, refrigerator, beds, clothes and many more things. Timo was able to go back once with his car but the car could only take so much. The children had pleaded, *"Papa biko wetalu ay akukwo ayi"*, Dad, please get our story books for us, so he made sure he got all the story books, toys and bicycles.

They fled to the safer parts of Biafra further away from the fighting. They and other people like them, who fled from their homes, were called "refugees". They kept moving from place to place in Biafra for safety.

The world heard about the Biafrans and their sufferings and reacted. People in the United States, United Kingdom, France, Germany, Israel, Italy and other countries in Europe donated money and food for the hungry Biafran children and their families. People from African countries such as Gabon, Ivory Coast, Tanzania and Zambia also gave their support to the suffering and struggling Biafrans.

There were also many volunteer aid workers who went to help the Biafrans in the refugee camps, tending to the sick and wounded and helping to feed the starving children. Many of these aid workers came from Ireland and because they were Catholic priests and nuns, they were known as the Irish Fathers and Sisters. Others came from other countries such as Britain, United States, France, Israel and Germany.

Soon, plane loads of food and medicine were being flown in by brave pilots into Biafra. As there was a war, Nigerian air force planes were shooting down any plane that went to Biafra and so these food aid pilots had to fly at night and land in the dark to avoid being shot down. Some of the planes carried weapons for Biafran soldiers too. Unfortunately, some were shot down and the pilots and aid workers killed. Those were really terrible times.

By 1970 the war ended. The Biafrans were very brave and fought very well, but the Nigerians had a much bigger army and more guns and in the end with the help of powerful countries like Britain and Russia they defeated the Biafrans. Many Biafrans were heart-broken but like Nigerians were relieved at last the war and the killings had come to an end. They became Nigerians again! Today, in Nigeria, there is still a lot of trouble in the country but it is still one country.

Marina and her family returned to their homes at Obosi and Onitsha at the war's end. They found that all their property had been looted, that is stolen. Many people found that their houses were found destroyed or damaged. Some found their houses already occupied by Nigerian soldiers. The children's school, All Saints Primary School had been bombed, shot at and the school library burnt. They were all sad but at least, the war was over and the killings and the hunger would stop. It is said that about 2,000,000 (two million) people or more died.

Throughout the war, Marina did not forget her children's education. She organised lessons and activities to keep them occupied. She got and gave them books to read and checked on their progress. When they came back to Nigeria, although they had lost about 2 years of schooling they did quite well in their new Nigerian school classes.

In Lagos where they moved to, they made friends quickly with other children from other parts of Nigeria who lived in Lagos and were not caught up in the war. Children can be really good at making friends and getting along no matter their nationality, ethnicity, religion or backgrounds.

And this was the case with Nigerian children after the war which was caused by bickering adults!

At some point during the war schools in the part of Biafra where they lived had re-opened and her children went back to school Although they were war-time schools and had little or no equipment, few books and no libraries, they were very welcome for Biafran parents. Biafrans valued education a lot and even when they were hungry or at war they still thought education was important. When the war ended, the Biafran children who returned to Nigeria were surprisingly very good in their classes. And so were Marina's children, her pride.

CHAPTER SIX

Peacetime: Family Ups and Downs
& Up Again

The Biafran war was also known as the Nigerian Civil War, because it was really a war between different parts of Nigeria. Those who were known as the Biafrans wanted to be free from Nigeria to live as they chose but the other Nigerians and the Nigerian government did not want them to leave...

A civil war takes place when different sides, groups or communities in the same country disagree and then fight a war over their disagreement. Many countries have had civil wars. There was the English civil war hundreds of years ago. There was the Spanish Civil war in the 1930s and a civil war in Russia in the early part of the 20th century. There have been civil wars in Sierra Leone, Congo, and China and so on.

There was also the American Civil war of the 19th Century. Like the Biafrans in Nigeria, the American Confederate States in the south wanted to break away from the United States and set up their own country but their reasons were very different from those of the Biafrans, and very wrong. The Biafrans wanted to leave Nigeria to escape the killings and persecution and have freedom to run their affairs, but the Confederates wanted to leave the United States so that they could carry on with slavery and the persecution of black people. President Lincoln and the Union Army were clearly the good guys and it was a good thing that they won.

When a part of a country breaks away from it and forms its own country that act is called secession. For example, the country Eritrea seceded from Ethiopia after a long civil war. Not all secessions or separations need a war to happen. Sometimes different parts of the same country agreed to separate, usually after a referendum. A good example of this is the country formally called Czechoslovakia. In 1993, the two main parts of the country agreed to separate and form two different countries. One is now called the Czech Republic and the other is now called Slovakia.

Not all secessions or attempts to secede are for good reasons. The Confederate attempt to secede from the United States, as already pointed out, was not for good or moral reasons. Wanting to maintain a state of slavery is simply wrong and evil. President Abraham Lincoln was right!

Being one of the good guys or having a good reason for secession does not mean that you will win or succeed. It is just the way things happen sometimes and sometimes good guys do lose. The Biafrans lost. When the war ended, many of the Ikeazor's friends who were on the other side and who were Nigerians were very anxious to see them. The war, like other civil wars, left many finding themselves on both sides. And throughout the war, many folks were very anxious for their friends and sometimes family who were caught up on the other side, especially in Biafra where things were extremely difficult. At the war's end, there was much bad news for those who found out that some of their friends had been killed or died, but there were also thousands and thousands and thousands of happy reunions between friends.

The Ikeazor's friends who were Nigerians had been very worried for them during the war as they knew a lot of people were dying. These friends invited them to their homes and celebrated their survival of the war. They helped them settle down to and adjust to being Nigerians again. Two of these very good friends were known to the children as Uncle Tanko and Uncle J.S. They were some of their father's closest friends and saw them as their uncles. Joseph Sarwan Tarka (JS) was from a part of Nigeria called Tiv Land. He was a famous politician and a campaigner for minority rights. He was, like Chimezie Ikeazor, a Christian. Tanko Yakasai was from another place called Kano, in the northern part of the country and he was a Muslim. Nigeria is a country that has people with different religions - Christians, Muslims and African belief followers.

Sometimes there is trouble between Muslims and Christians, especially in the Muslim northern parts of the country, but among these groups are still friends, very close friends, who care for each other regardless of their religions. The Ikeazors, Tarkas and Yakasais were from all different parts of Nigeria but it did not matter at all to their families. The men, the fathers, treated each other's children like nephews and nieces. Their wives carried on like sisters. They were stories of great friendship that the children, now older folks themselves, still tell to this day. It was also a story that could be found in many forms at the end of

46

many wars, friendships surviving the pains of war. The Ikeazors moved to Lagos, the Nigerian capital city then after the war and Marina's husband resumed his career as a Nigerian lawyer. His law practice was growing and he was becoming quite famous.

Nigeria, like every other country has rich and poor, but Nigeria is one of those countries where there are far too many poor and the poor are really having very tough times. The poor often have too little to eat, very poor education for their children, live in shanty towns or slums and have very little money to spare or buy things with. Sometimes, people will need the services or help of a professional like a doctor, architect, or lawyer and will have to pay for those services. Sometimes, when people are in trouble with the police or have been arrested they will need a lawyer to help with their matter. This may be to help them get the police to release them (on bail) or to speak for them in court before a judge.

Sometimes, some of Marina's family's neighbours or friends might need a lawyer and they would come to her husband. He would do some lawyer's work for them and they would pay him. Sometimes some of those neighbours may not have enough money to pay a lawyer but they would ask Marina if she could ask her husband to help them with some free work. She would ask him and many times he would agree. He liked saying "yes" to her and he had could be very kind-hearted to needy people too.

This went on for some time until they thought that the government should helping poor people who need lawyers when they are arrested or are in trouble with the law. This was the way it was in the United States, the United Kingdom, much of Europe and even in Zambia in southern Africa.

Marina and her husband had lived in England, where he studied law, for about four (4) years. They knew of a programme in England called Legal Aid. This programme provided anyone with legal advice and services, for free, whenever they were in trouble with the law and were arrested and taken to a police station.

This programme was paid for by the government. Marina and her husband had many conversations about why such a good programme should be set up in their country, especially for the poor. They also met a man called Mr. Osakwe who ran such a scheme in a small African country called Zambia. Marina's husband was really inspired by now and Marina wondered why a big and rich country like Nigeria could not have the legal aid programme when a much smaller country like Zambia had one.

Soon Marina's husband thought that he should ask the Nigerian Federal and State governments to set up a scheme for poor people in need of lawyers or legal services whenever they are arrested. Her husband was now known more as Chimezie rather than Timo or Timothy. Chimezie was his Igbo, African name.

In 1974, Chimezie set up a club for lawyers to give free legal aid to poor people in Nigeria. The club was called the Nigerian Legal Aid Association. It became a campaigning body for free legal aid in Nigeria. They travelled all over the country giving free legal aid to poor people arrested by the police or who were brought before the courts. They were also telling the state and federal governments to set up free legal aid programmes for the poor. After many years, the Nigerian government set up a Legal Aid department for the whole country. Marina's husband became even more famous. Everyone called him "The Poor Man's Lawyer". In 1979, the new Nigerian Constitution gave poor people the right to free legal aid. It was a historic step.

Things were going well for Marina and her family in the 1970s, all her children were at school and by 1974, and her first son had enrolled at a university to read law. By the late 1970s, four of her children, the last 2 boys and the 2 girls were in England at public school and her second son, Emeka, was at the Buckingham University reading accountancy.

The family now had a home in London and one in Lagos. Things were looking pretty good for Marina. One of her biggest dreams was for all her children, boys and girls, to go to university and gain degrees. High school was certainly not enough. They had to go to university. It did not matter if it was the boys or the girls. It was all the same for her. Her husband, Chimezie, shared her views too. Boys and Girls should have equal rights to education.

As far as Marina and Chimezie were concerned, there was no question of their daughters being off to marry as teenagers or before they had completed their university education. The importance of education was drummed into the children's head. They knew where they were going from very early. Marina and her husband bought their children lots of toys, toy cars, train sets, dolls and so on and plenty of books as well. Their house was filled with story books. The children also had plenty of

48

people in their family who had gone to colleges and universities and this made it all seem quite normal and expected.

One of their father's half-brothers was a doctor in Germany and another was a lawyer in Lagos. He would later become a judge. Marina's younger sister was already a doctor, by the early 1970s. They had cousins and family friends who were university graduates, authors, doctors, accountants, engineers and so on. Even their great-great grandfather who had died long before they were born was a writer.

Everything around them at home, in their family, in their parents' friendships, in their family history and the Nigerian attitude towards education encouraged them. Nigerians were generally very respectful of people who were very educated. Many Nigerians worked very hard to give their children good education.

Marina spent a lot of her time managing the affairs of all her children from a parent's point of view. When it was school holidays in England she would travel to London to be with her children who would come home to the family home during school break. Sometimes she would take them on short breaks around the country or to Europe.

She would sometimes bring them back to Nigeria to join their older siblings who were in Nigeria. At Christmas time, the whole family would travel over 300 miles by road back to Obosi to visit and spend Christmas with family and friends there. At Obosi lived the children's grandmothers, uncles, aunts, cousins and other friends. They also had aunts, great aunts, cousins and friends at Onitsha.

At this time, she and her husband were really getting on very well. In 1972, they returned to England together for the first time since their student days. They took their first two children, Emeka and Chukwudum with them. They had plenty of sights to see and plenty of visiting to do.

There were cousins, friends and a father to see. A grandfather too. Her husband's father, the former police man now lived in England and so Marina, her husband (his son) and their two sons went to visit him at his house at 130 Norwood Road in Tulse Hill, South London. It was a very happy reunion. They had not seen the old man since 1964 when he retired from the police and went to London to live.

The two children were extremely happy to see their grandfather again. They used to go his house in Enugu in Nigeria for holidays when they were very little boys. The older boy so admired his grandfather and he did say; "I want to be a policeman when I grow up". It was the sort of things kids everywhere said and maybe no one took him seriously, but that little boy did really grow up to become a police man, first in Nigeria like his grandfather and later on in England. That was Ada's dad, Chukwudum.

The tourists also went to visit a woman who was very important to Mr. and Mrs. Ikeazor in their student days in the 1950s. This was Joan Battershill, their landlady who had become Marina's stand-in mum when she was a homesick teenager. Aunty Joan was extremely delighted to see Marina again after so many years. They chatted away late into the night and when the Ikeazors were about to leave, Marina and Chimezie, who had already discussed it said to Joan Battershill, "We are having you over in Nigeria for a holiday next year!"

Mrs. Battershill was shocked with surprise and thrilled with joy as she hugged them both. And indeed the following year, Joan Battershill was invited to Nigeria by the Ikeazors for a multi city, multi village, sightseeing all expenses paid trip to Nigeria. They never forgot that kind Welsh woman and she never forgot them either or her first ever and fantastic trip to Africa.

In 1979, after many years of being ruled by soldiers, who should not really run countries, Nigerians had an election and elected a president, vice president, several governors and hundreds of legislators. They were exciting times and Marina's husband joined a political party.

With so many different things goings on and after some arguments, Marina and her husband started growing apart. They tried to fix things and make up but it did not work especially because other people got involved with her husband. By 1981, her husband left her for another woman. He stopped communicating with her. This was very hurtful for Marina.

Their marriage had only a few years earlier and since their wedding been thought of as the "perfect marriage" because they seemed so happy together and had six bright children and her husband was wealthy and famous. As they say there is really no such thing as a "perfect marriage". And as a Nigerian song goes, "No Condition is Permanent".

Although Marina and her husband were not divorced, Marina's husband could marry again- though not at a church or court registry. Nigerian laws and customs allowed for a man to have more than one wife - two, three or even four or more. The practice of having more than one wife, polygamy, happens in many parts of Africa and Asia, because the culture, laws or religions allow it.

It is against the law in many other countries, such as all the European countries and today in the United States. Being married to more than one person at the same time is bigamy and in many countries such as the United Kingdom and United States, a person could be sent to jail for that.

In the United States, many years ago, the Mormons, in the State of Utah practiced polygamy but were forced to stop by American laws. There are all kinds of arguments for polygamy, usually by men, but it is generally not a good idea for life in the modern day.

It is not fair on women. Men do not want to share their wives with other men so why should women anywhere have to share their husbands with other women? Any more than one wife for a man or any more than one husband for a woman brings a lot of confusion and complications so marriage should really be between one man and one woman at the same time and not more!

Marina's husband could not marry his new wife in a church or court house because he did not have a proper and lawful divorce from Marina. So, he had to settle for what Nigerians call traditional or customary marriage where men were allowed to have more than one wife. This may seem very odd to Britons, Europeans or Americans but it is not strange in many parts of Africa and Asia. The current President of South Africa, Jacob Zuma, has several wives!

Marina and her husband were fully separated by 1981 and no longer lived in the same house. Her husband and his new wife had 4 children and he had his own new family and unfortunately no longer paid any attention to Marina and his other children. It was very sad for them but life had to go on and some of them like the first two were no longer boys anyway. They were now young men.

Marina was now having a very hard time. She had been a housewife all the time and did not have any job. Although two of her sons had just finished from university, she still had young children, teenagers, to put through school. She felt very abandoned by her husband who would not speak to her or ask after her. Things were really very difficult for her but she had faith in God. She prayed a lot and asked for wisdom and help. She also knew that prayer alone would not fix things for her and that she had to work to raise money.

In many parts of Africa and some parts of regions like Asia, it is seen as seen as important for a woman to have a husband in her life whether or not there is love in the relationship. A lot of respect is attached to a woman just because she is married and some seem to be taken from her just because she is not married, separated or divorced.

In a modern world, every woman deserves respect whether she is single, married, separated or divorced, just as single, married, divorced or separated men do. Men and women are equal before the law in countries with modern laws. They all have equal rights and being married or not and being a man or woman should have nothing to do with people's rights or right to be respected.

After Marina's separation or what can be described as abandonment by her once loving husband, she had a lot of sympathy from some folks. These people thought she was treated very badly and unfairly. On the other hand, some people treated Marina very badly and some who were once friends walked away. Phone calls and visits from some slowly dried out as did invitations to family events. Some she knew before were disrespectful to her and others made silly comments about her and her children.

She no longer had a car or driver and for many years did not even have her own home. Some of her husband's relatives and his wife and her relatives and friends were unkind and rude to her and even made fun of her for being abandoned by her husband. Spiteful things were said about her and her children. They were made very unwelcomed in their father's home in many ways, for example by not being provided for, offered a bed or room to stay or simply told they were not welcome outright. Marina was powerless, but remained calm, prayerful and hopeful.

Marina was hurt by her husband's attitude towards her and the behaviour of some of his relatives, his new wife and her friends. There was nothing she could do other than to ignore them, do her best to avoid those who upset her, continue praying to God for wisdom and patience and continue raising her children the best she could. She was very concerned about her children's education and knew that her savings would run out some time.

In the early years of the separation she used to cry a lot but she tried very hard not let her children see her crying. It always distresses children, young and old to see their parents crying and Marina did not want to distress them or add to their sadness about the family break up.

If only Marina had gone to university when she was young and studied for a profession. If only she had learned a trade and had a paying job things may have been a little different for her now. If only she was a teacher, accountant, civil servant or like her younger sister, a doctor, or had a shop or market stall.   Her experience stressed the importance of education and employment for women.

She was totally devoted to her husband and to the children and in fact, being a mother was a fulltime job. It was a very important job too; it was just that you did not get paid money for that job. You get paid with thousands and thousands of "thank yous" and lots and lots of love and the joy of the job!

Sometimes when Marina was very sad about being left by her husband, her children would give her pep talks. Of course, they gave her lots of money when they started working but money is not everything. The younger ones, especially Chimezie and Nonso were extremely affectionate towards her and gave her plenty of hugs and cuddles at any time. She just told them, *"If you really want me very happy, just do well in your education and make sure you go to university"*. And they did.

The older children, especially Emeka and Chukwudum were not so affectionate. They were older and more practical. Marina's children now became her advisors and counsellors. Whenever she got very sad especially during the more difficult years they would tell her things like *"You are very blessed - you have six children and they are all well, alive and working hard"*. This would remind her of her blessing and good fortune. One of them would tell her that *"every storm that has a beginning has an end"* and another would say a very well-known proverb, *"behind every cloud is a silver lining"*.

By this time Marina's young sister, Edna, who had been a doctor for a few years was also able to give Marina a lot of help. Until she was able to rent her own home, Marina stayed with her sister and her family at their apartment, for as long as she needed. With the help of some good and loyal friends, such as Brigadier and Mrs. Kpera of Benue State, she started a cement selling business. She would go to a cement factory in a city called Markurdi, buy many bags of cement and then sell on to traders and building merchants. She did it for a few years and with the money she made she able to support those of her children who were still in education and pay rent on the house she rented.   By the late 1980s at least four of her children had finished from university and were working.

53

They all started helping their mother in one way or the other and things became much easier for her.

Meanwhile, her husband became even richer and more famous. He was well known throughout the country as a top lawyer. He had a great life and had several cars. He and his wife threw frequent parties at their home at Obosi and travelled to Europe for holidays very often. He and his new wife now lived at Obosi in a massive mansion attended by an army of cooks, servants and drivers. By 1986, he was appointed a Senior Advocate of Nigeria (SAN) and became one of the country's most senior lawyers.

In England, lawyers who held that sort of rank were called Queen's Counsel or QCs. He and his wife were millionaires by now or at least lived like millionaires, but he still did not extend any hand to Marina for their children's school fees or upkeep. In Nigeria, the rich man was all powerful and being a very top lawyer made him even more powerful. There was nothing that Marina could do to get her husband pay monies to her such as what is called Child Support or Child Maintenance payments in the UK or the USA.

The situation was also very embarrassing for her and her children and really a family scandal. Most people do not want to broadcast to the public their family difficulties or any scandal and Marina and her children were no different. By the 1990s all her children were working. Some lived in England and some lived in Nigeria and Marina now soon started dividing her time between Nigeria and in England visiting and staying with her children.

In the late 1990s there was an attempt to reconcile Marina and her husband. He seemed happy with it at the time but soon seemed to bow to some pressures and changed his mind. After many people at Obosi thought that reconciliation had at last come to their favourite couple, her husband did a U-turn and the whole peace process fell apart. They never reconciled again and he died in 2012.

When her husband died, his first son, Chukwudum and Ada's dad gathered all his father's children and the two wives, and with the support of his siblings, Emeka, Nwamaka ad Sharon, he ensured that the whole family including the wives were reconciled. Profuse apologies were offered and acceptance eventually returned. A lot of wrong had been done and a whole lot of hurt caused but folks have to learn to move on sometimes.

In November 2012, the entire family united to give their grand old man Chimezie Ikeazor, the Oboli III of Obosi, a befitting funeral in the Obosi traditional way. There was not one moment of dissent or dispute at the event, to the surprise of many people. Chimezie Ikeazor was 82 when he passed away. He was a very important man in the country. He was one of the most senior lawyers. He was an elder and a chief in his hometown. He was the recipient of national honours, but above all he was remembered affectionately as the poor man's lawyer. His funeral was a massive communal affair and attracted thousands of people from all over the country.

By the 2000s things were very different for her compared to the early 1980s when her husband left her. She now had absolutely no money worries. Beside her own, she had six homes (her children's homes) in England and Nigeria where she could go and come as she pleased and she did, travelling all over the place!

She had 12 grandchildren across five countries in three continents. She is a busy grandmother! There is a birthday phone call to make almost every month of the year, a card to send and a present to wrap. On her birthday, August 13 phone calls will be streaming in to her from near and far.

This year, she will be 80 years old. That is 8 decades of an adventurous and experience filled life that resulted in six children, twelve grandchildren and scores and scores of friends all over the world.

Marina in afro, a 1970s popular hairstyle

CHAPTER SEVEN

Sisters Who Reached for the Stars

Even though her education was stopped when she was a schoolgirl by her father, in accordance to prevailing attitudes, Marina maintained a keen interest in education. She loved reading novels and story books as well as the Bible. She also read newspapers as much as she could and kept herself informed of whatever was going on. She was very much interested in the wider world beyond whatever town she lived in.

After she got married and when she returned from England she looked at her younger sisters and wondered if they too will be married before they completed their education.

Her sisters were very bright but her father had the same ideas as he did for her. Her father now had three wives and had more than 12 children. In Nigeria, education was not free and parents had to pay for their children's education right from the nursery, through primary school, all the way to university or wherever they stopped. Sending many children to school could be very expensive and so some parents with many children could only afford to send only a few or some to school sometimes and sometimes only up to primary school or secondary school.

If Marina's father, Benson, had one wife and may be three or four children, he might have been a very wealthy man because he was well paid in his job and retired with a good pension. But now he had 3 wives and 12 or more children and lots and lots of school fees and pocket money and other expenses to think about. His daughters knew he supported their education but only up to secondary school. Anything further and university was for boys and they knew their father would set aside some money for that. The girls were expected to marry after secondary school or what Americans call high school. This happened in many families. The girl there were even lucky as in some parts of the country, up north, many girls did not even get to go to school at all.

Marina said to her father that her sisters must go to university if they wanted to. She spoke to her sisters and half-sisters and many of them wanted to go high school and university. She encouraged them. She would give them some money and some of her clothes and shoes and buy them books. She said quite firmly to them, *"I don't want to hear anything about marriage until your education is done".* Her sisters got the message and they had thirst for education anyway.

Her father agreed that they would go to high school but he was not so sure about university. He said it was too expensive and that it was better to keep money for boys' education rather than girls'. Marina said that when they were ready for university that something will be figured out but that they must be in education.

Edna the Doctor:

Marina's husband totally supported her in her views and helped to encourage her sisters. One of them wanted to be a doctor and took entrance examinations for the medical school at the University of Ibadan. It was a tough and very competitive examination but she passed! Her name is Edna and she was a very bright student. Marina was very happy. Her husband was very happy and so was her father.

Edna was happy to be at university. It was the first time in her life that she had ever been so far from her parents – some 300 miles or so. She was also taking wonderful steps in fulfilling her ambition to become a doctor. She also knew that Marina's own ambitions were being realised through her. She was at the university for only two or three years when the Biafran war broke out and she had to abandon her studies to flee home. Many parts of Nigeria were no longer safe for Edna's people at that time. During the Biafran war, many medical students were used as medical assistants or even junior doctors and Edna was going to be very useful in Biafra.

Many people were sick and injured and there were just never enough doctors and nurses. Edna then became one of the medical assistants or trainee doctors. She helped to treat people who were wounded by bombs and bullets or who were sick from malnutrition.

Many of her patients did not know the difference and called her and other medical students "doctor". There was no rest for them throughout the war. Besides a few days taken off to get some rest when they were exhausted, the doctors and medical student assistant worked throughout the entire war. They were helped by many doctors and nurses from foreign countries in Europe and North America.

A group of those foreign doctors and medical helpers that came from France, later formed an international medical charity organisation, at the end of the war. The charity is now world famous and is known as Medecin sans Frontier, which in French means Doctors or Medicine without borders. They travel to anywhere there is conflict or need for medical assistance and help the injured and wounded free.

By the time the war ended, the young medical student now in her mid-twenties had gained a lot of experience in practical medicine even before she became a fully qualified doctor. She returned to her university medical school at Ibadan and even though she had lost 3 years of medical studies and re-started at her pre-war grade, she was the most experienced student in her class. By 1973 she qualified as a doctor and was one of the best students in her graduating class.

She was now Dr. Edna Onyire. She was the first female doctor from her hometown Obosi. Marina was very pleased and proud of her little sister, Dr Edna. Marina's children were proud of their aunt who was now a "doctor". She later on went to the famous Medical School at the University of Edinburgh, in Scotland to study some more. A few years later, Edna married a fellow doctor, Iroha Iroha. Yes, Iroha was his first name and also his last name! They went on to have two children, a boy and a girl. Both were treated equally and both went on to go to university, read medicine and become doctors. Marina's little sister is now a doctor, married to a doctor and is the mother of two doctors.

Uche the Lawyer:

Marina has several other sisters some of whom went on to university. One of them went on to become a lawyer. Her names are Uche and Beatrice. She was called "Beattie" by all her family although she later preferred her African name "Uche", when she went to University. Today, as a lawyer, she is known by all her colleagues and friends as "Uche", while her family including her nephews and nieces still call her "Beattie" (pronounced be-ah-tee), simply out of habit of so many years.

When she was young, Marina was her idol, her big sister who had been to England, married a lawyer, was a great cook, dressed smartly, could drive and had six lovely children. In those days, at Onitsha (and this was

59

the early 1960s), it was very rare to see a woman drive or even wear trousers.

During her school holidays, she would come and stay at Marina's house and help around. That was the African way. By her mid-teens Uche was in the middle of her secondary education. Some of her classmates left school when they "found" husbands (that means a man proposed to them or a marriage was arranged). Uche would stay to complete her education. Marina who did not complete hers was now a looming figure who ensured that nothing would disrupt her kid sisters' education.

During her high school, when she was in her teens, there were marriage enquiries from other families about her and a good number of interested young men, including a certain dashing Army Captain. It was quite normal for another family to send word to another that they were interested in a young girl for their son who may have shown interest. With Marina's strong stand, all those enquiries were replied with the explanation that Uche was in school and would finish her education first before considering marriage.

Marina always told her sisters in school "You must finish your education first before any talk or thoughts of marriage" and by that she meant at least secondary school education which Americans call High School. Marina made sure their old father understood this too so that they would not be married off at 16 or 17 and be quitting school. Uche was very attached to her big sister and she liked helping her out with looking after her children. When the war broke out, Uche and other members of her family fled to the same place of refuge with the Ikeazors. Marina's husband was providing for many of them. Uche and other relatives lived with her and her family. She helped with the cooking and looking after the children and she also helped out her husband as his law clerk and assistant.

When the war ended she also came to Lagos with them. When she finished her secondary school education she started working with Marina's husband as an assistant and later as manager in his law firm. From there her interest in law continued to grow and by 1974 with Marina's support and very active support from Edna she enrolled at the University of Nigeria, Enugu to read law. By 1979 she had graduated from university, completed a year at law school and was called to the bar. She was now a fully qualified lawyer.

Probably the proudest person at her call to bar ceremony (lawyers' graduation ceremony) was Marina. Their mother, Elizabeth Nwudenkwo, at Obosi was also extremely proud too. She now had a daughter who was a doctor and another who was a lawyer, a barrister.

Very sadly, her husband and their father had died in 1970 and did not live to see his daughters graduate from university. Uche later married a doctor and had six children all of whom are graduates and some like their mother, are lawyers. She is a corporate lawyer in Lagos today.

And what about Marina's brothers?

Her brothers did not do badly either. One of them, Anene, joined the Nigeria Police and rose to become an Assistant Commissioner of Police by the time he retired. Sadly, he passed away in 2016. Her lastborn brother, Nnamdi, whose mother was her father's last wife, went on to follow in Edna's footsteps to read medicine. He is now a Professor of Medicine at a medical school in Nigeria. Her other brothers and sisters pursued various and different paths with most of them going to university to read one course or the other. Sadly, however, over the years a number of her siblings died.

Marina, mother, grandmother, matriarch – mid 2000s.

CHAPTER EIGHT

The Six Pack (Her Children)

Between 1956 and 1967 Marina and her husband had six children, four boys and two girls. Some of these six were later to have their own children, giving Marina 12 grandchildren by 2013! Here are short accounts of where and when they were born and who they are.

Chimezie

The last of the bunch is Chimezie who was born in October 1967. He is the only one of the six who was born in Biafra and he is very proud of that. He was born at the city of Owerri to the sound of gun fire, bombing and air raids.

He lives in London. He is a graduate of the University of Warwick where he gained degree in philosophy in 1992.

Nonso

Nonso was born at Onitsha, the city with the largest market in Africa, in January 1966. He went to Sherburne Prep in Dorset with younger brother, Chimezie, in the 1970s and studied law at the University of Nigeria. He is now solicitor at criminal law practice in London.

Sharon

Sharon is the second of the two girls. She was born at Obosi at her grandmother's maternity clinic in August 1961. She read law at the University of Benin, in Nigeria and is a barrister, following in her father's footsteps. She is presently the head of the Pensions Directorate in Nigeria.

Nwamaka

The first of the pair of girls is Nwamaka. She was born in Lagos in 1960: a year after her parents came back from England. She went to the same schools as her younger sister Sharon but went to Ahmadu Bello University where she read Graphics Design. She lives in Lagos where she runs the Ethnic Heritage Centre, an art and cultural activities hub. She was the first girl to be born in over a generation in the entire Ikeazor family at Obosi and her birth was roundly celebrated. She is the Ada of the family, the head of all the Ikeazor females everywhere!

Emeka

Emeka was born in September 1957 at Obosi, like his father before him. He was born in his grandmother's maternity home. Before the Biafran war, he attended All Saints Primary School with three of his siblings and after the war he went to St Gregory's College in Lagos. He studied accountancy at the Buckingham University in England. He is a bank chief executive in Lagos.

Chukwudum

Like his younger brother, Chukwudum was born in September, but a year earlier in 1956. He is the oldest of the six-pack and was born when his parents were students. He attended All Saints Primary School Onitsha and St Gregory's College Lagos. He is a retired police officer and lives in London where he is a bookseller.

****

When her first son, Chukwudum graduated from university in the mid-seventies, Marina was very happy but never for a minute thought that it was enough. There were five more children and she wanted all of them to go to university too and of course to graduate. There was no difference in how the boys and the girls were treated over their education. They all had the best their parents could afford and were encouraged to go all the way.

So, one after the other they kept going to university to read subjects of their choice. Finally, in 1992 her last child, Semo graduated from the University of Warwick where he studied philosophy. He had made has mother very happy when he finally agreed and enrolled in the university in 1989. With that Marina now felt satisfied at last as far as education was concerned. She was a very happy mother and soon a happy grandmother as her grandchildren, nieces and nephews too began to go to university and graduate. Today, some are doctors, architects, lawyers, bankers and so on.

And now, the grandchildren

From 1985 to 2013 Marina became a grandmother 12 times! Each time any of her children had a child she became a grandmother all over again. She loved it. In 1985 Marina became a grandmother for the first time. Her daughter Sharon had a baby boy, Abraham and so Marina's first grandchild was also a grandson.

Her last grandchild is Ikenna, Chukwudum's son and Ada's brother, who was born in Atlanta in August 2013. Her grandchildren are scattered all over the world as their parents live in different countries or they have gone to distant and different countries to study. Today, she has grandchildren in Sweden, Nigeria and the United States. One of them is thirty and one is just three!

The story is probably not over as more may yet be on the way.

This is the full and up to date list of Marina's grandchildren.

1	Abraham (Abie)		Architect, Abuja, Nigeria
2	Nnenna		Banker, Lagos
3	Olisa		Student, Atlanta, Georgia
4	Nnamdi		Student, Washington DC, USA
5	Somkene		Student, Georgia, USA
6	Obinna		Student, Stockholm, Sweden
7	Kaito		Student, Lagos, Nigeria
8	Ifeoma (Ify)		Student, Stockholm, Sweden
9	Dumebi		Military Cadet, Tennessee, USA
10	Ezinne		4th Grader, Lagos, Nigeria
11	Ada		3rd Grader, Georgia, USA
12	Ikenna (Ike)		Pre- Kindergarten kid, Georgia.

CHAPTER NINE

The Matriarch Today

Today Marina lives in Lagos. She spends a lot her time receiving visitors, visiting others, gardening and reading. She also loves cooking, especially for her children and grandchildren and their friends. Her granddaughter, Ada, who tasted African / Nigerian food for the first time in 2010 when she visited and stayed with her grandmother in London, still asks after her grandmother's dishes.

Marina's grandchildren in Lagos all love her cooking and love trooping to her house for all kinds of treats. Many times, when they visit, they take their friends along with them. She can also make her children and grandchildren laugh a lot with her behaviour and jokes. She can tell you the same story or the same jokes three times in month as if it was the first time and is full of funny stories from the past. She is a mixed bag of opinions with likes and don't likes like everyone else.

For example, she is not crazy about football or sports but she watches it sometimes, especially the world cup. For some reason, her favourite team is Western Germany. She refused all attempts to remind her that the country is simply called Germany today. She supports them in the World Cup unless they are playing against Nigeria. Her favourite footballers are Franz Beckenbaur, Eusebio and Pele. This tells that she is really very old as these people stopped playing football decades ago!

She likes the Queen a lot, that is, Queen Elizabeth of England and thinks she is one of the best things about the United Kingdom. The Queen was the queen when Marina first came to England in 1955 as a teenager! Marina was not too keen on the younger generation royalty like Princess Diana and Fergie, but she thinks Princes William and Harry are great fellows. And as for young people, she thinks that the Pakistani school girl, Malala is the bravest of the brave and admires her greatly. Well, every right thinking person must!

When she was young her favourite TV programmes were Peyton Place and I love Lucy but now she likes to watch the English soaps EastEnders, and Downton Abbey. Her favourite Nigerian show was the soap, Village Headmaster, which ran in the 1970s and 1980s.

Her favourite female politician is Golda Meir of Israel because she thinks she was a strong ruler at a time when there were few female national leaders. She also liked Indira Gandhi and used to tell her children about her when they were young. Her favourite political leader is Nelson Mandela, but then is that not so for many people?

In her younger days, some of her favourite artists were Millicent Small (who sang "My Boy Lollipop") and the Seekers. She also listened to classical music with her husband and her favourite composer was and still is Mozart. She also listened to Nigerian artistes like Victor Uwaifo, Celestine Okwu and Rex Lawson. When she was young, things like Music CDs and iPods were non-existent and unimagined. Music was played on vinyl records only.

She likes many aspects of Igbo and African cultures and their many ways of doing things such as family life, extended family, respect for elders, support for each other, the rich foods, beautiful clothes and so on but she strongly disagrees with any part she thinks is unfair and unjust. She thinks that men and women, boys and girls must have the same right to education. She also is very much against polygamy, the idea of men marrying more than several wives at the same time. It is doubtful if any woman will think it is a brilliant idea.

She is a Christian as her parents were. She was brought up in the Anglican tradition, what Americans would call Episcopal, but she attends any Christian church happily; Catholic, Anglican, Baptist, or Pentecostal and sings along with the rest of the church. Although she is Anglican, she is very familiar and fond of the Catholic tradition because she went to a Catholic Covent school when she was a girl.

She has Christian, Muslim, Atheist, African belief friends and relatives. Through her children and grandchildren has also come to know many people from many parts of the world and different religious beliefs, Hindus, Jains, Jewish people, Buddhists and so on. She thinks that it is crazy that people should fight over religion or that some people should try to force others to change their religion. She does not preach to anyone about religion and believes in respecting other people's choices.

Recently, some troubles broke out in some of the northern parts of Nigeria where some religious group wanted to force other people to follow their beliefs by force. There was a lot of violence and bombings causing the death of many people and hardships hundreds of thousands who had to leave their homes. In 2012, this group kidnapped nearly 300 schoolgirls from their school because they did not believe that girls should go to school.

Marina has been very saddened by all these as the sufferings of the ordinary people reminded her of the Biafran war refugees. The kidnapping of the little girls from their schools was also a reminder that even in the 21st century there were still people who, for religious reasons, believe that girls should not be educated.

Still, Marina has seen a lot of changes in her life. She has seen the times when women in her country simply were not expected or encouraged to go to college and university to a time when women accountants, lawyers, police officers, professors, doctors, judges, legislators, even commissioners of police are all around, despite of some negative attitudes still in some places.

She is proud of her children and grateful to them for fulfilling her ambition for them to go to university. She always told them, "It does not matter what you want to do, just get some good education in your pocket first". As far as she was concerned, some of the best presents they could give her when they were children was good school examination results.

An avid traveler, she does not let her age get in her way. She frequently shuttles between England and Nigeria, all by herself and has travelled similarly within Nigeria visiting family and friends across the country. She has been on cruises across the Mediterranean and the Caribbean visiting places like France, Spain, Jamaica and the Bahamas. She has visited at least, 20 out of Nigeria's 36 states. At 80, there is no stopping her!

She has homes in Lagos, Obosi, Abuja, and London. Actually, her only real home is her house in Lagos, but in those cities mentioned her children have homes and mostly reserve a room for her for her frequent and long stay visits. Sometimes she spends as much as three months or more in London. When in Nigeria, she divides up her time between Lagos, which has been her home for decade, and her ancestral hometown, Obosi.

Family is very important in many African cultures as it is for many people all over the world. Many of her travels have to do with family – her children. She enjoys travelling to various places where her children and grandchildren live. In 2010, she came to England for a very important reason. That was the year she met her granddaughter Ada, Maya who is also named Marina. That is the granddaughter who has commissioned this book.

At 80, she is now the elder of the family, the matriarch. . She is a respected and adored by her family and community who regard her as a great achiever by virtue of her children and charity to others.

Her children, grandchildren, siblings and an army of nieces and nephews and their friends adore her and spend a lot of time trying to spoil her in any way they can.

Well, they should. She deserves it. Well done Marina and Happy 80th birthday!

GLOSSARY

Biafra

The name of the republic that tried to break away from Nigeria in the 1960s. The civil war that broke out in Nigeria during that period is also known as the Biafran War. Up to 2,000,000 people were killed in that war.

Civil War

Armed conflicts or wars between two or more sections or groups in the same country are described as civil wars.

Extended Family

The family beyond parents and children to include grandparents, uncles, aunts, and cousins.

Igbo

A people in Nigeria, a country with up to 200 different communities and languages. The Igbo are an ethnic community or nationality much the same way as the Welsh or Scots, are with their own culture, language and portion of territory they occupy. Other peoples or ethnic communities in Nigeria include the Ijaw, Efik, Tiv, Edo, Idoma, Igala, Ibibio, Yoruba, Jukun, Hausa and Fulani.

Lingua Franca

A common language spoken by people with their own different languages. In the United States, English is the Lingua Franca as it is in Nigeria.

Matriarch

A matriarch is a female head of a family, usually an elderly person or the oldest member of the family.

Nigeria

The largest country in terms of population in Africa. It estimated to have a population of over 180 million. It is home to over 200 different ethnic communities with as many languages. Some famous people from Nigeria or who have Nigerian ancestry are Wole Soyinka, a Nobel Prize Winner,

71

Sophie Okonedo, an Oscar winning actress, Chimamanda Adichie, the author, the late Chinua Achebe, the world famous writer and the late Hogan Bassey and Dick Tiger, former world boxing champions.

Patriarch
This is the exact opposite of matriarch as this is a male head of the family or clan.

Polygamy
The practice of marrying and having more than one wife or husband at the same time. The practice is usually about men marrying more than one wife.

Refugees
Refugees are people who have fled their homes to another part of the country or another country because of war or persecution.

RECOMMENDED READING

Life Among the Ibo Women of Nigeria (1998)
by Salome Nnoroviele

Children Just Like Me: A new celebration of children around the world (2016) by Catherine Saunders.

Chike and the River
by Chinua Achebe

Let Me Tell You About My Family and the Ocean City (2015)
by Adaeze Ezeani.

Schools Around the World (Children Like Us)
by Moira Butterfield

Amazing World Atlas: Bringing the World to Life (2014)
by Lonely Planet Kids.

I Am Malala: How One Girl Stood Up for Education and Changed the World: Young Readers Edition (2016)
by Malala Yousafzai

Without A Silver Spoon
by Eddie Iroh

Refugees and Migrants (Children in Our World) 7 Oct 2016;
by Ceri Roberts (Author), Hanane Kai (Illustrator)

Dear Grandma, from you to me : Memory Journal capturing your Grandmother's own amazing stories Diary – (2007)
by Neil Coxon

How it Works: The Grandparent (Ladybirds for Grown-Ups); 2016
by Jason Hazeley (Author), Joel Morris (Author)

INDEX

Lightning Source UK Ltd.
Milton Keynes UK
UKOW06f1812020817
306563UK00001B/6/P

9 781999 764203